Best of Graphis
Photo I

D1410801

PAGE

PAGE ONE PUBLISHING

In the case of some of the reproductions in this book it proved impossible to locate the originals, despite careful research. They were, however, considered to be of such importance that the decision was taken by the present publisher to reproduce from other published sources.

Coverphotographer : Robert Mapplethorpe

© 1993 by Graphis Press Corp., Dufourstrasse 107, CH-8008 Zürich, Switzerland

© 1993 for this edition by Page One Publishing Pte Ltd., Singapore
Distributed worldwide by Könemann Verlagsgesellschaft mbH, Bonner Str. 126, D-50968 Köln

Designed by Peter Feierabend, Berlin
Text: Ansgar Pächter, Cologne
English translation: Michael Hulse, Cologne
French translation: Michèle Schreyer, Cologne

Printed in Singapore
ISBN 981-00-4768-1

Foreword

Most of the photographs in this book were taken for publicity purposes. The people in them chose their own self-dramatizing poses or obeyed the instructions of the photographers, whose ideas seem inexhaustible. To think of the effort a whole team puts into pictures like these! The finding of props! To be plain about it, I am none too keen on these kind of photos myself because they seem too pushy. Their posed artificiality is loud. But they capture my attention – thus fulfilling the intention. And they are good examples of their kind.

It is difficult to do justice to these photographs as samples of a particular kind of picture. I would have to consider the circumstances in which each one was taken, who commissioned it, for what purpose. I would have to be sure of the idea that fired each picture. Rather than do this, I propose to examine two photographs and a sequence that appeal to me directly (not because they seize my attention but because I like them) and which I find easy to assess without recourse to categories of technique, art, reportage or advertising. These have nothing to do with the impact of the photographs on me.

The first (p. 24) is an advertising shot for Hasselblad, a three-quarter length portrait of the star violinist Anne-Sophie Mutter. She is facing us frontally, head bowed, eyes closed, apparently absorbed with herself. She is holding her instrument, which hangs vertically and marks the lower perimeter of the picture. Her dark jacket with its emphatically horizontal shoulderline and plunging cleavage are a strong geometrical contrast to the softness of her face and the flowing lines of her lips. This woman, conveying an effect of great modesty here, is in fact remarkably charismatic.

The second photo (p. 63) shows seven monks in their monastery, positioned unusually. They are all wearing long, pale cassock habits and make a very serious impression. A votive painting on the rear wall, and wooden benches along the sides, suggest that they are in a hall of prayer or a refectory. The windows are about ten feet above floor level, allowing light into the room but not permitting a view of what may be outside. Except for one monk seated on the right to the rear, in the shadow, they are all facing us, looking at us. It is as if they knew our doubting question – "What are they doing there?" – and were offering a confession with a mere look. (The picture was commissioned by the Sunday Times magazine and will presumably have been published in a reportage context – but what difference does that make?)

Finally I should like to draw attention to a group of four photographs (p. 83), two above and two below, that comprise a square rich in inter-relations. The pictures are personal work on the subject of transience, youth and age combined with the relations of the sexes. Simply to identify this subject matter is of course to interpret. The photographer gave no title to his pictures. To my mind, the photos primarily require to be read from top to bottom, and the most powerful emotional charge is carried by the picture at bottom left, where the father (who else?) who once dandled his boy on his knee is now, old and frail, being carried by his son, like a child. It is an image of love, fresh and unstereotyped.

How are we to respond to the tidal wave of images that everyone speaks of? My own feeling is that one should stay calm and take one's time. This book contains a number of photographs that merit that courtesy.

Vorwort

Die meisten der in diesem Band gezeigten Photographien sind Werbephotographien. Die porträtierten Personen inszenieren sich in selbstgewählten Posen oder folgen dem Arrangement der Photographen, denen die „guten Ideen" nie auszugehen scheinen.

Ich stelle mir den Aufwand vor, den da ein ganzes Team betreibt, dieses Herbeischaffen irgendwelcher Requisiten... Kurz und gut: Ich mag solche Photos nicht so gern, weil sie mir zu aufdringlich sind. Ihr artifizieller Charakter ist dröhnend. Sie nehmen meine Aufmerksamkeit in Anspruch. – Also erfüllen sie ihren Zweck! Und gut gemacht sind sie auch.

Als Exemplare eines bestimmten Typs von Photographien kann ich diesen Photographien nicht gerecht werden. Ich müßte sie einzeln betrachten und dabei berücksichtigen, von wem und für welchen Zweck sie jeweils in Auftrag gegeben wurden. Ich müßte mir die hinter jedem Photo stehende Idee klarmachen. – Viel lieber aber konzentriere ich mich hier auf nur zwei Photographien und eine Photosequenz, die mich unmittelbar ansprechen (nicht weil sie Aufmerksamkeit fordern, sondern weil sie mir gefallen) und bei denen es mir leicht fällt, von allen Aspekten drumherum wie „Werbung", „Reportage", „Kunst" und „Technik" abzusehen. Diese haben nichts mit der Wirkung der Photos auf mich zu tun.

Bei dem ersten Photo (S.24) handelt es sich um eine Kamera-Werbephotographie für Hasselblad: ein Dreiviertelporträt der Violinenvirtuosin Anne-Sophie Mutter. Dem Betrachter frontal zugewandt, hat sie den Kopf leicht gesenkt und wirkt – mit ihren verschlossenen Augen – ganz in sich gekehrt. In ihren Händen hält sie, senkrecht nach unten herabhängend, ihr Instrument, das das Photo unten begrenzt. Ihr dunkles Jackett mit ausgeprägt waagerechten Schulterpartien und tiefem V-Ausschnitt bildet einen deutlichen geometrischen Kontrast zu den weichen Linien ihres Gesichts und der schön geschwungenen Form ihrer Lippen. Die Ausstrahlung dieser Frau, die sich hier den Anschein der größten Bescheidenheit gibt, ist bemerkenswert.

Das zweite Photo (S. 63) zeigt eine eigenartig angeordnete Gruppe von sieben Mönchen in einem der Innenräume ihres Klosters. Sie tragen lange, helle Talare und wirken sehr ernst. Ein hochformatiges Heiligenbild an der den Raum nach hinten abschließenden Wand sowie an den Längsseiten angebrachte Holzbänke lassen auf einen Gebetsraum oder das Refektorium schließen. Die Fenster beginnen erst in etwa drei Metern Höhe, so daß sie dem Raum zwar Licht geben, aber jeden Blick nach außen verwehren. Bis auf einen Mönch, der rechts hinten im Schatten sitzt, sind die anderen dem Betrachter zugewandt und schauen diesen an. Es ist, als wüßten sie um dessen ungläubige Frage – Was machen die da? – und wollten durch ihren Blick ein Bekenntnis ablegen. (Auftraggeber des Photos war das Sunday Times Magazine; es fand vermutlich im Rahmen einer Reportage Verwendung. Aber spielt das eine Rolle?)

Abschließend möchte ich die Aufmerksamkeit des Betrachters auf eine Gruppe von vier Photographien lenken (S. 83), die, je zwei Photos oben und unten, zu einem beziehungsreichen Viereck angeordnet sind. Es handelt sich dabei um eine freie Arbeit, die das Thema Werden und Vergehen, Jungsein und Altern, mit dem Thema der Geschlechterbeziehung verbindet. Schon die Benennung dieser Themen ist natürlich eine Interpretation, der Photograph hat seinen Photos keine Titel gegeben. Die Hauptleserichtung der Photos ist m.E. die von oben nach unten. Die stärkste emotionale Botschaft geht für mich von dem Photo unten links aus: Der Vater (wer sonst?), der einst seinen kleinen Sohn auf dem Schoß hielt, wird nun, alt und gebrechlich geworden, von diesem auf den Armen getragen wie ein Kind – ein noch unverbrauchtes Bild der Liebe.

Wie ist der vielbeschworenen Bilderflut zu begegnen? Meine Empfehlung lautet: Ruhe bewahren und sich für wenige Bilder Zeit nehmen. Dieser Band enthält mehrere Photos, die diese Zeit verdienen.

Préface

La plupart des photos présentées dans cet album sont des photos publicitaires. Les personnes reproduites se mettent en scène dans des poses qu'elles ont choisies ou suivent les directives du photographe, jamais à court de bonnes idées, semble-t-il.

Je me représente tout le déploiement d'énergie que cela représente pour une équipe, les accessoires à aller chercher... Bref, je n'aime pas tellement ce genre de photos, car elles me semblent s'imposer trop au spectateur. Leur caractère artificiel est tonitruant. Elles exigent mon attention – donc elles remplissent leur objectif! Et en plus elles sont bien faites.

Je ne peux pas juger objectivement ces photos car elles sont des exemplaires d'un certain type de photographies. Je devrais les regarder une à une et prendre en considération qui les a commandées et dans quel but. Je devrais comprendre l'idée qui se trouve derrière chaque photo. Mais je me concentre ici beaucoup plus volontiers sur seulement deux photographies et une photoséquence qui m'intéressent directement (non parce qu'elles exigent de l'attention mais parce qu'elles me plaisent) et à la vue desquelles il me paraît facile d'oublier les aspects qui les entourent tels que «publicité», «reportage», «art» et «technique». Ils n'ont rien à voir avec l'effet que les photos ont sur moi.

La première photo (p. 24) est une photographie publicitaire pour une caméra Hasselblad: c'est un portrait en trois-quarts de la violoniste virtuose Anne-Sophie Mutter. Tournée vers le spectateur, elle a la tête légèrement penchée et semble – ses yeux sont clos – plongée en elle-même. Elle tient son violon qui pend verticalement devant elle et sous lequel la photo s'arrête. Sa veste sombre, aux épaules horizontales soulignées et au profond décolleté en V, forme un contraste nettement géométrique avec les lignes douces de son visage et ses belles lèvres incurvées. Le rayonnement de cette femme, qui se donne ici l'apparence de la plus grande modestie, est remarquable.

La seconde photo (p. 63) montre un groupe de sept moines placés bizarrement dans une des salles de leur monastère. Ils portent de longues robes claires et semblent très sérieux. La représentation haut format d'un saint, sur le mur qui clôt la pièce à l'arrière-plan ainsi que des bancs de bois le long des murs nous donnent à penser que la pièce est un oratoire ou un réfectoire. Les fenêtres sont placées à trois mètres au-dessus du sol, de manière à laisser entrer la lumière mais à ne pas permettre le regard sur l'extérieur. A l'exception d'un moine, assis derrière à droite dans l'ombre, les autres sont tournés vers le spectateur et le regardent. On dirait qu'ils connaissent sa question incrédule et muette – Que font-ils là? – et voudraient se confesser du regard. (Le Sunday Times Magazine avait commandé cette photo; elle a probable-ment été utilisée dans le cadre d'un reportage. Mais est-ce important?)

Pour conclure je voudrais diriger l'attention de l'observateur sur un groupe de quatre photographies (p. 83), qui, deux en haut et deux en bas, sont disposées en un carré riche en correspondances. Il s'agit ici d'un travail libre qui associe le thème «devenir et passer, être jeune et vieillir» au thème des rapports entre les sexes. Nommer ces thèmes, c'est déjà les interpréter, le photographe n'a pas donné de titre à ses photos. Pour bien les lire, me semble-t-il, il faut les lire de haut en bas. Le message le plus puissant au niveau émotionnel se dégage pour moi de la photo en bas à gauche: le père (qui d'autre) tenait autrefois son petit garçon sur ses genoux, aujourd'hui qu'il est vieux et infirme, son fils le porte comme un enfant – l'Amour en une image qui n'a pas encore perdu son pouvoir d'expression.

Quelle est la marche à suivre face à ce flot d'images? Je conseille de rester calme et de prendre son temps pour n'en regarder que quelques-unes. Cet album contient des photos qui méritent qu'on leur consacre cette attention.

Mark Seliger
Mark Spitz, swimmer

Mark Seliger
Heavy metal jewelery

Mark Seliger
John Lee Hooker, musician

Mark Seliger
John Lee Hooker, musician

◁ △ Jean-Paul Goude
Grace Jones, singer

Jean-Paul Gaude

Jean-Paul Goude
Portrait of Carolina

Sandi Fellman
LaDormeuse, 1982

Sandi Fellman
Penna, 1983

Sandi Fellman
Chorus I, 1985

Sandi Fellman
Merlin's Prophecy #2, 1982

Sandi Fellman
In The Night, 1982

Sandi Fellman
Untitled, 1986

Klaus Mitteldorf
Morami

Untitled

Klaus Mitteldorf
Untitled

Untitled

 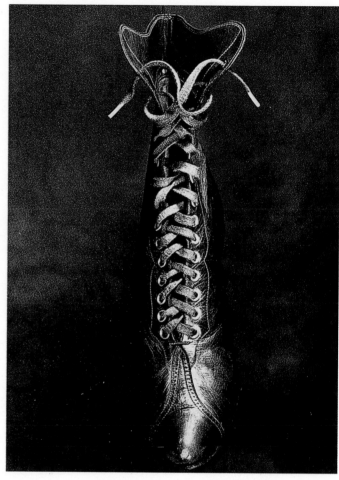

Albert Watson
Russia

Albert Watson
Jewelery

Christian Vogt
From a "Sleep" calendar

Christian Vogt
Cigarette advertising campaign

Christian Vogt
Portrait of Anne-Sophie Mutter

Christian Vogt
Ilford calendar and
Hasselblad advertisement

Eric Watson
Record sleeve

Robert Mapplethorpe
Photo Japon

Matt Mahurin
Texas Prison

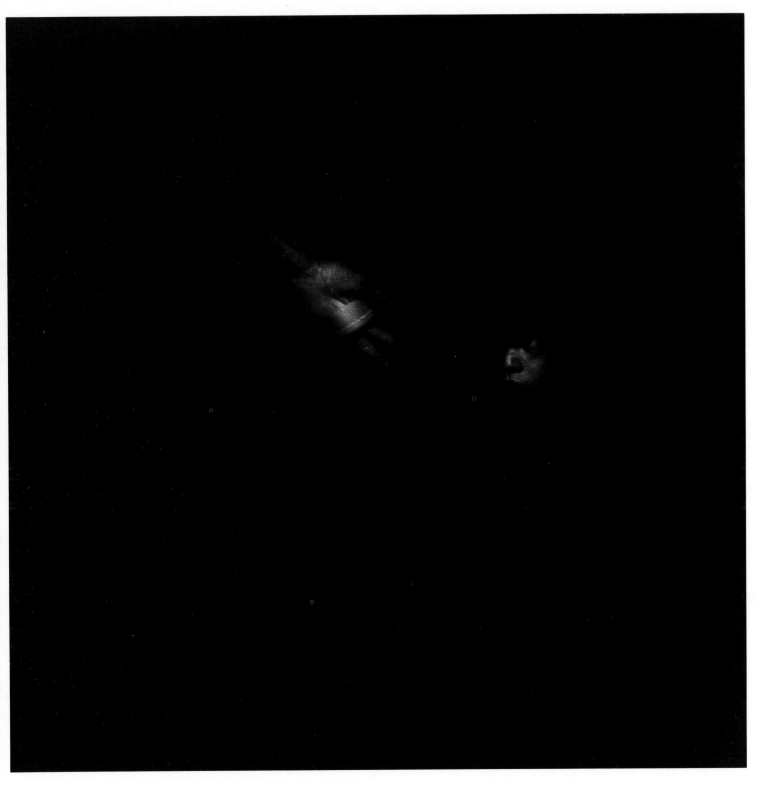

Matt Mahurin
Nicaragua

Matt Mahurin
Untitled

Matt Mahurin
Boxing gymnasium, New York City

Matt Mahurin
Paris

Matt Maharin
Madrid

Matt Mahurin
Texas prison

Matt Mahurin
Texas prison

Matt Mahurin
Paris

Matt Mahurin
Nicaragua

Matt Mahurin
Texas prison

Matt Mahurin
Texas prison

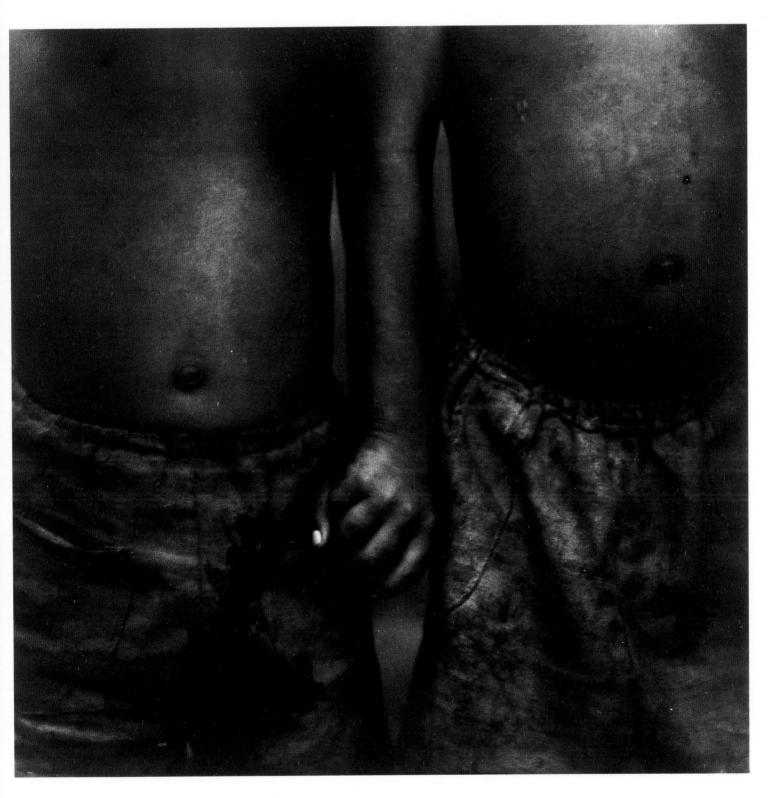

Matt Mahurin
Nicaragua

Jody Dole
Glass

Jody Dole
Salt and pepper

Jody Dole
Still life on white linen

Jody Dole
Cone

Jody Dole
Personal study

Jody Dole
Van briggle with red gladiola

Nana Watanabe
Personal work

Nana Watanabe
Bloomingdale's (for Christian Dior)

◁△ Nana Watanabe
Personal work

Hiro
Richard Avedon, photographer

Hiro
Bryan Adams, rock musician

Hiro
Martha Graham, dancer/choreographer

Hiro
Ed Harris, actor

Hiro
Popping pills

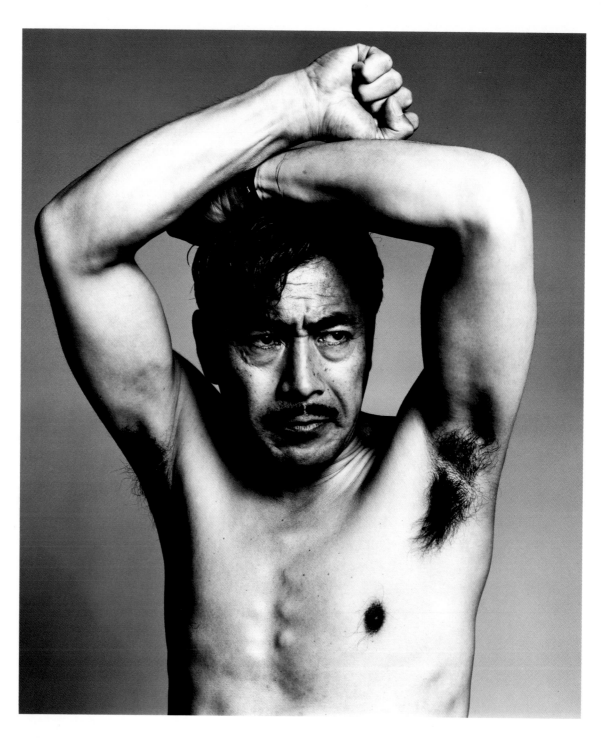

Hiro
Toshiro Mifune, actor

Hiro
Jerry Hall

Hiro
Eva Voorhis

Hiro
Pat Maguire

Hiro
Daniella Ghione

© 1987 American Express Travel Related Services Company, Inc.

Annie Leibovitz
Eric Heiden, olympic speed scater

48

Annie Leibovitz
Willie Shoemaker, jockey; Wilt Chamberlain, basketball player

© 1987 American Express Travel Related Services Company, Inc.

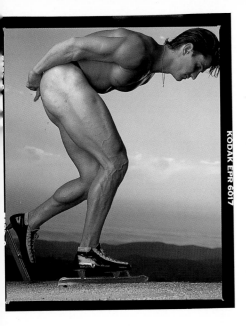

Eric Heiden
Olympic speed scater

Tip O'Neill
Former U.S. congressman

Elmore Leonard
Author

Quincy Jones
Record producer

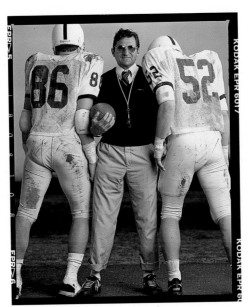

Joe Paterno
College football coach

Beth Henley
Playwright

Ray Charles
Musician

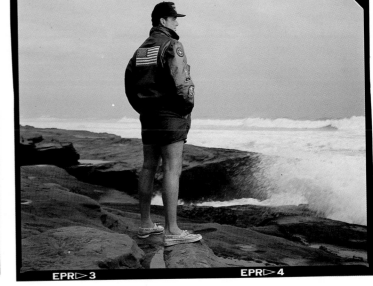

Beth Henley
Playwright

Dennis Conner
America's Cup winner

Hans Neleman
Ballerinas

Hans Neleman
Teaching a stone to talk

Hans Neleman
Still life with butter

Hans Neleman
Still life with cheese

◁△ Joyce Tenneson
Fashion photographs

Joyce Tenneson △ ▷
Personal work

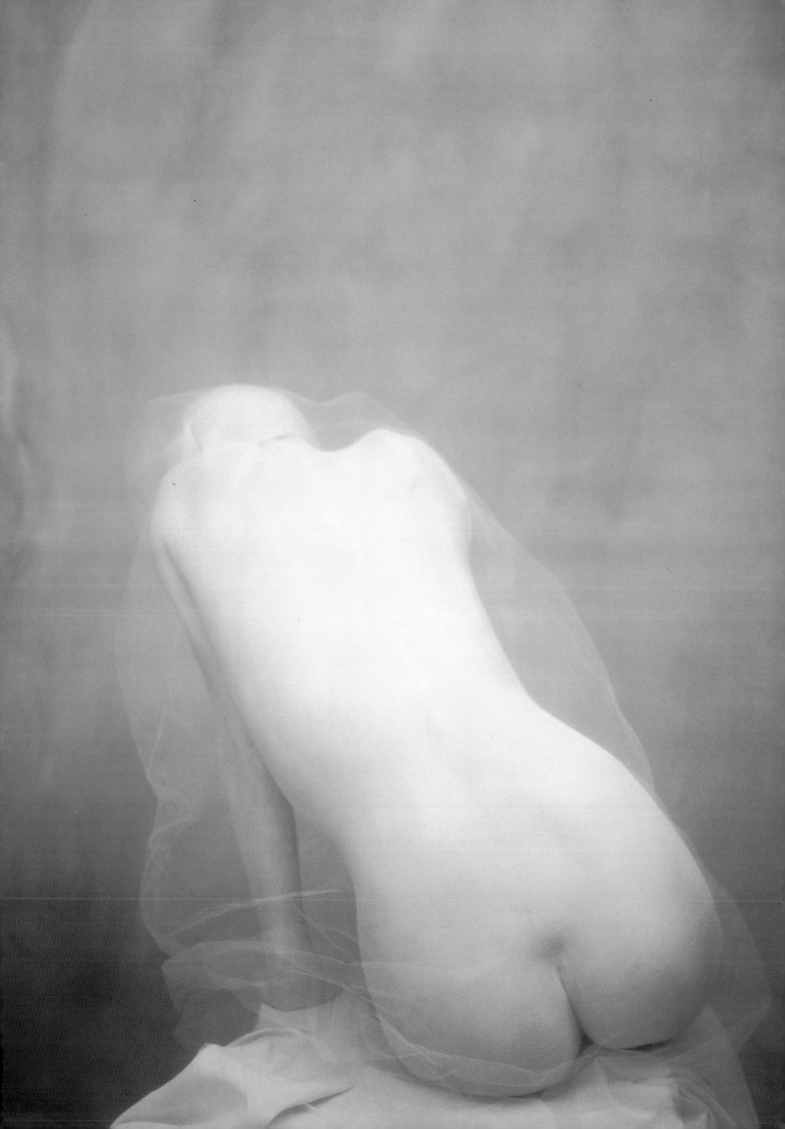

Aernout Overbeeke
Oak Alley, Louisiana

Cape Frehel, France

Aernout Overbeeke
The Ardennes by night

Millington, Tennessee

Aernout Overbeeke
The theatre group Caroussel

Aernout Overbeeke
The monks of the Abdij van Berne

François Hugier/VU
Contact

François Hugier/VU
Contact

Hans Namuth

Jean-Marc Tingaud

Paolo Calia

Agnès Bonnot / VU

◁ △ Jean Lariviere

Terry Heffernan
Design

Terry Heffernan
BMW hood

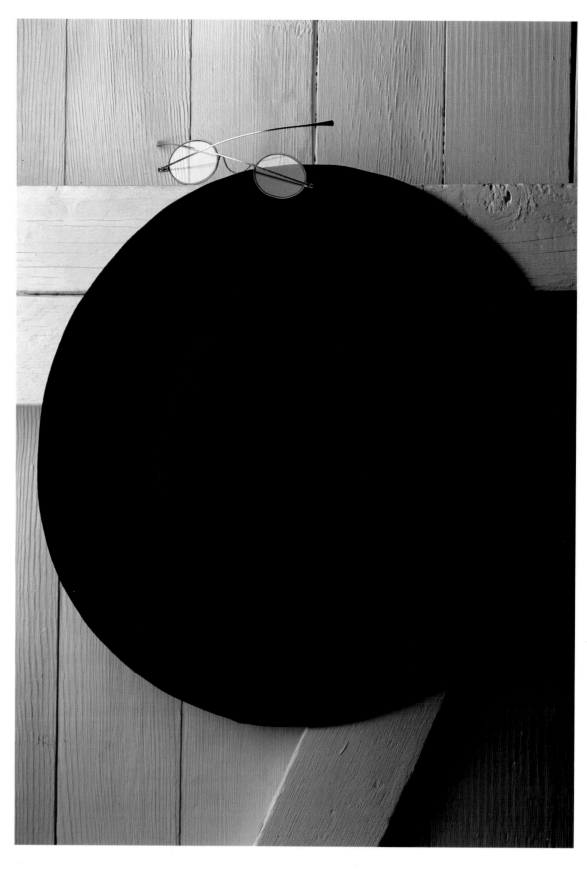

Terry Heffernan
Amish

Terry Heffernan
Woman behind screen door

Klaus Frahm
Flowers

Klaus Frahm
Flowers

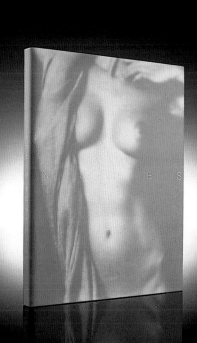

G R A P H I S   B O O K S

Photo '93 is a compilation of over 300 images selected from a world-wide call for entries. □ **Graphis Typography 1** spans the years from the "founding fathers" of type design through the modern masters. A comprehensive time line, examples of computer aided type design and pictorial displays of past and present designers make this book invaluable. □ **Design '94** a classic Graphis annual with 700 examples of visual communication spanning 256 pages with such categories as design, illustration, advertising, brochures, letterheads and more. □ **Poster '93** contains over 400 images and 256 pages and features introductions by Ron Dumas: Creative Director/Graphic Designer of Nike footwear, Makoto Saito, Japanese poster illustrator and Catherine Bürer of the Swiss Poster Collection. □ **Graphis Nudes** with 224 pages and over 200 images, this book is an elegant and impressive collection of carefully

selected images by the world's outstanding photographers. □ **Graphis Annual Reports 4** features the best in annual report design from fiscal 1991 and 1992. These reports are selected based, not only on outstanding design style, but also for excellence in photography, illustration and over-all composition. □ **Letterhead 2** is suited to guide and inspire the graphic designer in creating strong visual identities. □ **Graphis Paper Specifier System (GPS)** includes cross referenced indexes organized by paper manufacturer and paper name, region of merchant directory and factual paper information. □ **Logo 2** extensive in scope, the book is packed with over 300 innovative top-quality logos, created for both large and small firms, as well as not-for-profit foundations and organizations. □ **Photo '93** ist eine Sammlung von über 300 Bildern, die auf Grund ihrer künstlerischen Qualität

anlässlich des neusten internationalen Graphis-Wettbewerbs ausgewählt wurden. □ **Graphis Typography 1** bietet ein breites Panorama der Schriftgestaltung, von den Anfängen der Typographie bis hin zu Schriften, die mit dem Computer entwickelt wurden. Eine zeitliche Übersicht führt von den «Gründervätern» zu den modernen Meistern, dokumentiert durch zahlreiche Abbildungen. □ **Design '94**, der Klassiker der Graphis-Jahrbücher, zeigt weit mehr als 700 Beispiele visueller Kommunikation (Gestaltung von Broschüren, Anzeigen, Zeitschriften, Briefköpfen etc.). 256 Seiten Design total. □ **Poster '93** enthält über 400 Bilder. Eingeleitet wird der 256 Seiten starke Band mit Texten von Ron Dumas, Creative Director/Graphic Designer für Nike-Schuhe, von Makoto Saito, dem japanischen Plakatkünstler, und von Catherine Bürer, Direktorin der

Plakatsammlung des Museums für Gestaltung, Zürich. □ **Graphis Nudes** versammelt auf 224 Seiten 200 sorgfältig ausgewählte Aktphotos von hervorragenden Photographen aus aller Welt. □ **Graphis Annual Reports 4** zeigt Jahresberichte für 1991 und 1992. Beurteilt wurde die Gestaltung, aber auch die Qualität von Illustrationen und Photographie sowie der Produktion. □ **Letterhead 2** bietet Anregung und Inspiration bei der Gestaltung ausserordentlicher visueller Erscheinungsbilder. □ **Graphis Paper Specifier System (GPS)** enthält Papiermuster sowie Indexe nach Herstellern und Papiersorten, Händlerverzeichnisse und Angaben zu den Papieren. □ **Logo 2** zeigt ein breites Spektrum von 300 innovativen, hervorragenden Logos für kleine und grosse Betriebe, Institutionen und Organisationen. □ **Photo '93** est un recueil

de plus de 300 illustrations choisies pour leur qualité artistique à l'occasion d'un concours international. □ **Graphis Typography 1** présente un panorama exhaustif du design typographique, des pionniers de l'ancienne génération aux plus grands créateurs actuels. Vous y trouverez aussi bien des exemples de typographies élaborées sur ordinateur que des créations de designers d'hier et d'aujourd'hui. □ **Design '94** présente plus de 700 exemples de communication visuelle (création de brochures, d'annonces, de publications, de papiers à entête etc.). □ **Poster '93** contient plus de 400 images. La préface de cet ouvrage de 256 pages est signée par Ron Dumas, directeur artistique et graphiste de la marque de chaussures Nike, Makoto Saito, le créateur d'affiches japonais, et par Catherine Bürer, conservatrice de la collection d'affiche du Museum für Gestaltung à Zurich. □ **Graphis**

Nudes rassemble sur 224 pages 200 des plus belles photos des grands photographes contemporains. □ **Graphis Annual Reports 4** présente le meilleur des rapports annuels de 1991 et 1992. Les rapports sont choisies essentiellement en fonction de leur composition, mais aussi pour leur valeur sur le plan de photo ou du dessin et leur qualité de production. □ **Letterhead 2** offre aux graphistes une source d'inspiration pour la création de fortes identités visuelles. □ **Graphis Paper Specifier System (GPS)** contient des échantillons de papier ainsi qu'un index des fabricants et des différentes variétés de papier, un annuaire des représentants ainsi que diverses informations. □ **Logo 2** présente un vaste éventail de 300 logos pleins d'innovation et de très haute qualité conçus pour les entreprises de toutes tailles ainsi que pour les organisations à but non-lucratif. □

D I E   I N T E R N A T I O N A L E   G R A P H I S - R E I H E   D I R E K T   V O M   V E R L A G

K-93

GRAPHIS TITEL:

□	3-85709-293-9	**GRAPHIS PHOTO 93**		SFr. 123.--	DM 149.00
□	3-85709-463-2	**GRAPHIS TYPOGRAPHY 1**	(FEB. 93)	SFr. 137.--	DM 162.00
□	3-85709-193-2	**GRAPHIS DESIGN 93**		SFr. 123.--	DM 149.00
□	3-85709-393-5	**GRAPHIS POSTER 93**		SFr. 123.--	DM 149.00
□	3-85709-435-4	**GRAPHIS NUDES**		SFr. 168.--	DM 168.00
□	3-85709-431-1	**GRAPHIS ANNUAL REPORTS 3**		SFr. 137.--	DM 162.00

□	3-85709-441-9	**GRAPHIS LETTERHEAD 2**	SFr. 123.--	DM 149.00
□	3-85709-445-1	**GRAPHIS COORPORATE IDENTITY**	SFr. 137.--	DM 162.00
□	3-85709-442-7	**GRAPHIS LOGO 2**	SFr. 92.--	DM 108.00

□ SCHECK LIEGT BEI (AUSGESTELLT AUF GRAPHIS VERLAG AG, ZÜRICH)
LEBEN SIE IN EINEM EG ODER EWR-LAND? DANN BITTE GESAMT-
BETRAG ZUZÜGLICH 5,5% MEHRWERTSTEUER AUF SCHECK EINTRAGEN.

□ BITTE STELLEN SIE RECHNUNG (VERSANDSPESEN ZUSÄTZLICH)

MEINE ADRESSE LAUTET:

FIRMENNAME:

NAME:

ADRESSE:

PLZ/ORT:

LAND:

BITTE EINFACH AUSSCHNEIDEN ODER FOTOKOPIEREN, IN EINEN UMSCHLAG STECKEN UND EINSENDEN AN:

G R A P H I S   V E R L A G   A G ,   P O S T F A C H ,   C H - 8 0 3 4   Z Ü R I C H ,   S C H W E I Z